Australian Animals

Kangaroos

A 4D Book

by Sara Louise Kras

PEBBLE
a capstone imprint

Download the Capstone 4D app!

- Ask an adult to download the Capstone 4D app.

- Scan the cover and stars inside the book for additional content.

When you scan a spread, you'll find fun extra stuff to go with this book! You can also find these things on the web at www.capstone4D.com using the password: kangaroos.00009

Pebble Plus is published by Pebble
1710 Roe Crest Drive, North Mankato, Minnesota 56003
www.mycapstone.com

Library of Congress Cataloging-in-Publication Data
Library of Congress Cataloging-in-Publication data is available on the Library of Congress website.
ISBN 978-1-9771-0000-9 (library binding)
ISBN 978-1-9771-0005-4 (paperback)
ISBN 978-1-9771-0009-2 (eBook PDF)
Summary: This text discusses kangaroos and their habitats.

Editorial Credits
Jessica Server and Clare Lewis, editors; Charmaine Whitman, designer; Jo Miller, media researcher; Laura Manthe, production specialist

Image Credits
Alamy: Juergen Sohns, cover; Dreamstime: Kazzadev, 11, Sain Alizada, 9; iStockphoto: CraigRJD, 13, 19, MaXPdia, 5; Minden Pictures: Yva Momatiuk and John Eastcott, 17; Shutterstock: deb talan, 7, Jeremy Red, 15, Nicole Patience, 1, Pawel Papis, 21

Design Elements
Shutterstock: Pyty (map), oksanka007

Note to Parents and Teachers

The Australian Animals set supports the national science standards related to life science. This book describes and illustrates kangaroos. The images support early readers in understanding the text. The repetition of words and phrases helps early readers learn new words. This book also introduces early readers to subject-specific vocabulary words, which are defined in the Glossary section. Early readers may need assistance to read some words and to use the Table of Contents, Glossary, Read More, Internet Sites, Critical Thinking Questions, and Index sections of the book

Printed and bound in China.
000309

Table of Contents

Living in Australia 4

Legs, Feet, and Tails 8

Eating and Drinking 14

Growing Up 16

Staying Safe 20

Glossary 22
Read More 23
Internet Sites 23
Critical Thinking Questions 24
Index 24

Living in Australia

Australia has mammals that hop up to 30 miles (48 kilometers) an hour. They are furry kangaroos using their big back feet.

World Map

Asia

North America

Europe

Africa

South America

Australia

N

W — E

S

Antarctica

Some kangaroos live
in Australia's hot bush lands.
The rest live in forests
and grasslands.

Australia Map

where kangaroos live

Legs, Feet, and Tails

A kangaroo's long back legs
are made for jumping.
Kangaroos can travel
far and fast.

9

Kangaroos' front paws have sharp claws. They use their claws to dig in the dirt.

Kangaroos have
big, thick tails.
They lean back
on their tails to balance.

Eating and Drinking

Kangaroos eat grass.

They can go a long time without water.

Eating grass gives kangaroos some of the water they need.

Growing Up

Kangaroos are marsupials.
Female kangaroos have
pouches on their bellies.
Their newborn babies
grow in the pouches.

Young kangaroos
are called joeys.

For up to 10 months, joeys stay
in their mothers' pouches.

Kangaroos live up to 20 years.

Staying Safe

Some kangaroos form mobs.

One male kangaroo
is the leader of the group.
He watches for predators
and keeps the mob safe.

Glossary

balance—to keep steady and not fall over

bush lands—a somewhat dry part of Australia where trees and shrubs grow

joey—a young kangaroo

mammal—a warm-blooded animal that has a backbone and hair or fur; female mammals feed milk to their young

marsupial—a kind of animal that carries its young in a pouch on its stomach

mob—a group of kangaroos that live together; each mob has up to 20 kangaroos

pouch—a pocket-like flap of skin

predator—an animal that hunts other animals for food

Read More

Ganeri, Anita. *The Story of the Kangaroo.* Fabulous Animals. Chicago: Capstone, 2016.

Riggs, Kate. *Kangaroos.* Seedlings. Mankato: Minn.: Creative Education, 2017.

Rustad, Martha E.H. *Baby Animals in Pouches.* Baby Animals and Their Homes. North Mankato, Minn.: Capstone Press, 2017.

Internet Sites

Use FactHound to find Internet sites related to this book.

Visit www.facthound.com

Just type in 9781977100009 and go.

 Check out projects, games and lots more at
www.capstonekids.com

Critical Thinking Questions

1. Where do kangaroos live?

2. What do you think is the kangaroo's most powerful body part? Why?

3. Where do baby kangaroos live?

Index

Australia, 4, 6
babies, 16
balance, 12
bush lands, 6
claws, 10
digging, 10
eating, 14
feet, 4
forests, 6
grass, 14
grasslands, 6
joeys, 18

jumping, 8
legs, 8
lifespan, 18
mammals, 4
marsupials, 16
mobs, 20
paws, 10
pouches, 16, 18
predators, 20
speed, 4
tails, 12
water, 14